C000217934

Classic

AMERICAN

Classic
AMERICAN

Home cooking from all over the USA

INTRODUCTION BY
ANNE MAGRUDER

ULTIMATE
EDITIONS

First published by Ultimate Editions in 1997

© 1997 Anness Publishing Limited

Ultimate Editions is an imprint of
Anness Publishing Limited
Hermes House
88-89 Blackfriars Road
London SE1 8HA

All rights reserved. No part of this publication may be reproduced,
stored in a retrieval system, or transmitted in any way or by any means,
electronic, mechanical, photocopying, recording or otherwise,
without the prior written permission of the copyright holder.

ISBN 1 86035 212 X

Publisher Joanna Lorenz
Senior Cookery Editor Linda Fraser
Project Editor Zoe Antoniou
Designer Ian Sandom
Illustrations Madeleine David
Photographers Karl Adamson, Edward Allwright, Steve Baxter,
Amanda Heywood and Michael Michaels
Recipes Carla Capalbo, Frances Cleary, Roz Denny, Christine France, Sara Gates,
Shirley Gill, Patricia Lousada, Norma MacMillan, Laura Washburn and Steve Wheeler
Food for photography Elizabeth Wolf-Cohen, Wendy Lee and Jane Stevenson
Stylists Hilary Guy, Blake Minton and Kirsty Rawlings
Jacket photography Thomas Odulate

Typeset by MC Typeset Ltd, Rochester, Kent

Printed and bound in Singapore

For all recipes, quantities are given in both metric and imperial measures, and, where appropriate,
measures are also given in standard cups and spoons. Follow one set, but not a mixture,
because they are not interchangeable.

Picture on frontispiece shows a selection of food typical to the American
Midwest, including Country Meat Loaf and Butternut Squash Bisque.

1 3 5 7 9 10 8 6 4 2

CONTENTS

INTRODUCTION

What is classic American cooking? The quintessential American food – the hamburger – is a native of Germany. Chilli con Carne, though it sounds spicy and foreign, is in fact considered a culinary travesty south of the Texas border. Pizza, pasta, quiche, fajitas and guacamole, while unquestionably foreign, are also right at home on most "American" restaurant menus.

The stereotypical American is a rugged pioneer shaped by and shaping the endless frontier. But what he wants to eat is much closer to home: mother's cooking. The early settlers, for example, are no exception. Although the Pilgrims were grateful for the Indians' gift of corn, which kept them from starving during their first winter in North America, they planted wheat as soon as possible in order to duplicate the English breads and puddings they craved. They also imported beef, pork and all kinds of comfort foods from England to keep the home fires burning. Plenty of indigenous foods – among them corn, beans, clams, peanuts, cranberries and pumpkins – worked their way into the American repertoire, but the tone was and remains simple and homespun.

America is a nation made up of immigrants, all longing for the cooking they grew up eating, and in large cities, especially on the coasts, almost any ethnic food is available, from Polish to Peruvian. But if this country is a melting pot of cultures, its immigrant foods remain doggedly faithful to their homey origins. Within a few years of settling here, each immigrant group has made sure the ingredients they love are available. In the community gardens and backyards of our cities, an Italian American fusses over fennel and tomatoes while his Vietnamese neighbour raises fresh coriander and mint. Farmers' markets and supermarkets also abound with the traditional foods of all cultures.

Those traditional foods have taken root, making America their home. Many Italian dishes – macaroni and cheese, spaghetti with tomato sauce – are now American classics. It is highly likely that in a century or so, after Vietnamese immigrants have settled more regions of the country, opening restaurants along the way, the aromatic noodle soup *pho* will show up in an all American cookbooks. After all, the classic American dish, gumbo – a highly seasoned seafood stew – was originally African.

Picture on right shows a selection of muffins, buns and tea breads, including cornbread in the centre.

A selection of Southwestern dishes, including chilli con carne, cheese, soured cream, guacamole and nacho chips.

There are also many regional differences in eating habits, and these play a large part in defining American food. Seafood has always been popular in the coastal regions, for example, where oysters, clams and lobsters are plentiful. This has helped to shape the culinary heritage of New England as well as California. A wide range of seafood is now available in most supermarkets.

In the Southwest, a unique style of cooking has developed over the years which draws on Native American influences as well as the Mexican culture south of the border. These "Tex Mex" dishes, such as fajitas, are dominated by ingredients such as corn, tomatoes, beans, and are flavoured of course by the hot chilli pepper. They are popular everywhere and are enjoyed in many different restaurants.

In the Southern states, the mix of culinary influences is particularly diverse. History, over the years, has created many differing influences in the area, brought by French and Spanish

8

settlers and African customs that were introduced through the slave trade. Combined again with Native American customs, this region has become home to many rich and tantalizing dishes, where Cajun food is perhaps the most well-known. Southern Fried Chicken has become particularly popular elsewhere.

The Northwest and Mountain states offer good hunting and fishing territory, which is also central to the American style of cooking. There are many hearty meat dishes, such as meat loaf, that are very popular. The vast farmlands of the Midwest, however, emphasize the importance of home cooking and baking, with their great fields of wheat and corn. Indeed, breads and cakes are now a way of life: delicious goods such as muffins, pies and cheesecake have become representative, to a certain extent, of the national cuisine. Home-grown ingredients remain very much at the heart of American cooking, as the popularity of the vast number of local farmers' markets, prominent in cities and towns everywhere, shows. Supermarkets also stock an enormous range of the ethnic foods that have become so much a part of America.

Basically, classic American cooking is whatever is cooking in American homes. The recipes in this book – with a few high-toned exceptions such as Oysters Rockefeller and Caesar Salad – are what is being served at barbecues, brunches and Sunday suppers all across the country. At first glance, it is a collection of exotic specialities – why else would Pork Fajitas exist alongside Gumbo or Quiche? Close up, you will see a trove of nostalgic foods that, though technically imported, are far from exotic. As bold, brash and pioneering as Americans may be, American cooks look homeward, deliciously, for comfort. It is such food that has become what is as American as Apple Pie itself.

Picture above shows a typical Thanksgiving scene.

BEEF CHILLI SOUP

A hearty dish based on a traditional chilli recipe. It is ideal with fresh crusty bread as a warming start to any meal.

INGREDIENTS
15ml/1 tbsp oil
1 onion, chopped
175g/6oz minced beef
2 garlic cloves, chopped
1 fresh red chilli, sliced
15g/¹/₂oz/2 tbsp flour
400g/14oz can chopped tomatoes
600ml/1 pint/2¹/₂ cups beef stock
375g/12oz/2 cups canned kidney beans, drained
30ml/2 tbsp chopped fresh parsley, plus extra to garnish
salt and ground black pepper
crusty bread, to serve

SERVES 4

COOK'S TIP
For a milder flavour, remove the seeds from the chilli before slicing.

1 Heat the oil in a large saucepan. Fry the onion and minced beef for 5 minutes until brown and sealed.

2 Add the garlic, chilli and flour. Cook for 1 minute, then add the tomatoes and pour in the stock. Bring to the boil.

3 Stir in the kidney beans and season well. Cook for 20 minutes.

4 Add the parsley and season to taste. Pour into individual soup bowls, sprinkle with chopped parsley and serve immediately with fresh crusty bread.

FRESH TOMATO SOUP

T his brightly coloured soup tastes best when made with meaty, flavourful Italian plum tomatoes. Serve it with plenty of fresh bread for a satisfying lunch, or sprinkle over some croûtons for a dinner party starter.

INGREDIENTS
25g/1oz/2 tbsp butter or margarine
1 onion, chopped
900g/2lb sun-ripened tomatoes, quartered
2 carrots, chopped
475ml/16fl oz/2 cups chicken stock
30ml/2 tbsp chopped fresh parsley
2.5ml/1/2 tsp fresh thyme leaves or
1.5ml/1/4 tsp dried thyme
75ml/21/2 fl oz/1/3 cup whipping cream (optional)
salt and ground black pepper

SERVES 4

1 Melt the butter or margarine in a large saucepan. Add the onion and cook for about 5 minutes until softened.

2 Stir in the tomatoes, carrots, chicken stock, parsley and thyme. Bring to the boil. Reduce the heat to low, cover the pan and simmer for 15–20 minutes until the carrots are tender.

3 Purée the soup in a vegetable mill. (Alternatively use a blender or food processor, then sieve to remove seeds.) Return the puréed soup to the saucepan.

4 Stir in the cream, if using, and reheat gently. Season with salt and pepper. Ladle into warmed soup bowls and serve hot, sprinkled with a little more thyme, if you wish.

BUTTERNUT SQUASH BISQUE

I f butternut squash is not available, make this dish with another variety of squash, including pumpkin.

INGREDIENTS
25g/1oz/2 tbsp butter or margarine
2 small onions, finely chopped
450g/1lb butternut squash, peeled,
seeded and diced
1.2 litres/2 pints/5 cups chicken stock
225g/8oz potatoes, diced
5ml/1 tsp paprika
120ml/4fl oz/¹/₂ cup whipping
cream (optional)
7.5ml/1¹/₂ tsp chopped fresh chives, plus
whole chives, to garnish
salt and ground black pepper

SERVES 4

1 Melt the butter or margarine in a large saucepan. Add the onions and cook for about 5 minutes until softened.

2 Add the butternut squash, chicken stock, potatoes and paprika. Bring to the boil. Reduce the heat to low, cover the pan and simmer for about 35 minutes until the vegetables are soft.

3 Pour the soup into a food processor or blender and process until smooth. Return the soup to the pan and stir in the cream, if using. Season with salt and pepper and reheat gently.

4 Stir in the chopped chives just before serving. If liked, garnish each serving with a few whole chives.

NEW ENGLAND CLAM CHOWDER

This tasty soup made from fresh clams is a firm favourite in New England – try it out and see if it becomes one of your favourites!

INGREDIENTS
48 small clams, scrubbed
1.5 litres/2½ pints/6 cups water
40g/1½oz/¼ cup finely diced salt pork
or bacon
1 onion, finely chopped
1 bay leaf
5 potatoes, diced
475ml/16fl oz/2 cups milk, warmed
250ml/8fl oz/1 cup single cream
chopped fresh parsley, to garnish
salt and ground black pepper

SERVES 8

1 Rinse the clams well in cold water and drain. Place them in a deep saucepan with the water and bring to the boil. Cover and steam for about 10 minutes until the shells open. Remove from the heat.

2 When the clams have cooled slightly, remove them from their shells, discarding any that have not opened. Chop them roughly, then strain the cooking liquid through a sieve lined with muslin and reserve it.

3 In a large saucepan, dry fry the salt pork or bacon until it begins to brown. Add the onion and cook over a low heat for 8–10 minutes until softened.

4 Add the bay leaf, potatoes and clam cooking liquid. Stir, bring to the boil and simmer for 5–10 minutes.

5 Stir in the chopped clams and continue to cook until the potatoes are tender, stirring occasionally. Season with salt and pepper to taste.

6 Reduce the heat to low and stir in the warmed milk and the cream. Simmer very gently for 5 more minutes. Discard the bay leaf, taste and adjust the seasoning. Serve sprinkled with parsley.

COOK'S TIP
If the clams have been freshly dug, purging helps to rid them of all sand and stomach contents. Put them in a bowl of cold water; sprinkle with 50g/2oz/½ cup cornmeal and some salt. Stir lightly and leave to stand in a cool place for 3–4 hours.

OYSTERS ROCKEFELLER

D on't be worried about preparing oysters – to open them up, just push the point of a strong-bladed knife a short way into the "hinge". Push down firmly. The lid should then pop open.

INGREDIENTS
450g/1lb fresh spinach leaves
115g/4oz spring onions, chopped
50g/2oz celery, chopped
25g/1oz/1/2 cup chopped fresh parsley
1 garlic clove
2 anchovy fillets
25g/1oz/2 tbsp butter or margarine
35g/11/4oz/1/2 cup dry breadcrumbs
5ml/1 tsp Worcestershire sauce
15ml/1 tbsp anise-flavoured liqueur
(Pernod or Ricard)
2.5ml/1/2 tsp salt
Tabasco sauce, to taste
36 oysters in their shells
thin strips of lemon rind, to garnish

SERVES 6

1 Wash the spinach well. Drain and place it in a heavy saucepan. Cover and cook over a low heat until just wilted. Remove from the heat and, when cool enough to handle, squeeze to remove excess water.

2 Put the spinach, spring onions, celery, parsley, garlic and anchovy fillets in a food processor or blender and chop finely.

3 Heat the butter or margarine in a small saucepan. Add the spinach mixture, dry breadcrumbs, Worcestershire sauce, liqueur, salt and Tabasco sauce to taste. Cook for about 1–2 minutes, then cool and chill until ready to use.

4 Preheat the oven to 230°C/450°F/Gas 8. Line a baking sheet with crumpled foil.

5 Open the oysters and remove the top shells. Arrange the oysters side by side on the foil (it will keep them upright). Spoon the spinach mixture over the oysters, smoothing the tops with the back of the spoon.

6 Bake for about 20 minutes, until piping hot. Serve immediately, garnished with lemon rind.

NEW ENGLAND CLAMBAKE WITH LOBSTER

An exotic combination of fresh seaweed and lobsters makes this a bake that will certainly impress your guests.

INGREDIENTS
fresh seaweed
salt
6 lobsters, 450g/1lb each
900g/2lb pickling onions, peeled
900g/2lb small red potatoes
36 small clams
6 sweetcorn cobs, husks and silk removed
225g/8oz/1 cup butter or margarine
45ml/3 tbsp chopped fresh chives

SERVES 6

1 Put a layer of seaweed in the bottom of a large deep saucepan containing 2.5cm/1in of salted water. Put the lobsters on top and cover with more seaweed.

2 Add the onions and potatoes. Cover the pan and bring the water to the boil.

3 After 10 minutes, add the clams and the sweetcorn. Cover again and cook until the clams have opened, the lobster shells are red, and the potatoes are tender. This should take 15–20 minutes.

4 Meanwhile, melt the butter or margarine in a small saucepan and stir in the chopped chives.

5 Discard the seaweed. Serve the lobsters and clams with the vegetables, accompanied by the chive butter.

17

BAKED STUFFED CRAB

A wonderful looking dish that is surprisingly easy to make. Serve it as a dazzling main course for a dinner party with salad and rice.

INGREDIENTS
4 freshly cooked crabs
1 celery stick, diced
1 spring onion, finely chopped
1 small fresh green chilli, seeded and finely chopped
75ml/5 tbsp/¹/₃ cup mayonnaise
30ml/2 tbsp fresh lemon juice
15ml/1 tbsp chopped fresh chives
25g/1oz/¹/₂ cup fresh breadcrumbs
50g/2oz/¹/₂ cup Cheddar cheese, grated
25g/1oz/2 tbsp butter or margarine, melted
salt and ground black pepper
fresh parsley sprigs, to garnish

SERVES 4

1 Preheat the oven to 190°C/375°F/Gas 5. Pull the claws and legs from each crab. Separate the body from the shell. Scoop out the meat from the shell. Discard the feathery gills and the intestines; remove the meat and coral from the body. Crack the claws and remove the meat.

2 Scrub the shells. Cut into the seam on the underside with scissors. The inner part of the shell should break off cleanly along the seam, enlarging the opening. Rinse the shells and dry them well.

3 In a bowl, combine the crab meat, celery, spring onion, chilli, mayonnaise, lemon juice and chives. Season with salt and pepper to taste and mix well.

4 In another bowl, toss together the breadcrumbs, cheese and melted butter or margarine.

5 Pile the crab mixture into the shells. Sprinkle with the breadcrumb mixture and bake for about 20 minutes, until they are golden brown. Serve hot, garnished with parsley sprigs.

CAJUN BLACKENED SWORDFISH

his spicy fish dish will bring a ray of Cajun sunshine into your home at any time of the year.

INGREDIENTS

50g/2oz/4 tbsp butter or margarine
4 swordfish steaks, about 175g/6oz each
5ml/1 tsp onion powder
5ml/1 tsp garlic salt
10ml/2 tsp paprika
5ml/1 tsp ground cumin
5ml/1 tsp each mustard powder
5ml/1 tsp cayenne
10ml/2 tsp each dried thyme and oregano
2.5ml/¹/₂ tsp salt and 5ml/1 tsp pepper
boiled rice, to serve
dill sprigs, to garnish

SERVES 4

1 Melt the butter or margarine and brush both sides of the fish steaks with it.

2 Combine all the spices, herbs and seasonings and coat both sides of the fish steaks with it, rubbing it in well. Then heat a heavy frying pan for about 5 minutes or until a drop of water sprinkled on the surface sizzles.

3 Drizzle 10ml/2 tsp of the remaining butter or margarine over the fish steaks. Add the steaks to the frying pan, butter-side down, and cook for 2–3 minutes, or until the underside is blackened.

4 Drizzle another 10ml/2 tsp melted butter or margarine over the fish, then turn the steaks over. Cook for 2–3 minutes more, until the second side is blackened and the fish flakes easily when tested with a fork.

5 Serve the fish on a bed of rice, garnished with dill and drizzle over the remaining butter or margarine.

SEAFOOD AND SAUSAGE GUMBO

hen you serve this meal, make sure that each person gets both seafood and sausage on their plate.

INGREDIENTS

1.5kg/3lb whole raw prawns

1.75 litres/3 pints/7¹/₂ cups water

1 onion, quartered

4 bay leaves

175ml/6fl oz/³/₄ cup oil

115g/4oz/1 cup flour

50g/2oz/4 tbsp margarine or butter

3 large onions, finely chopped

225g/8oz green pepper, chopped

2 large celery sticks, chopped

675g/1¹/₂lb kielbasa (Polish) or andouille

sausage, cut in 1cm/¹/₂in rounds

450g/1lb fresh okra, cut in

1cm/¹/₂in slices

3 garlic cloves, finely chopped

2.5ml/¹/₂ tsp fresh or dried thyme leaves

10ml/2 tsp salt

2.5ml/¹/₂ tsp ground black pepper

2.5ml/¹/₂ tsp ground white pepper

5ml/1 tsp cayenne pepper

Tabasco sauce (optional)

400g/14oz can chopped tomatoes

450g/1lb fresh crab meat

rice, to serve

SERVES 10–12

1 Peel and devein the prawns; reserve the heads and shells. Keep the prawns in a covered bowl in the fridge while you make the sauce.

2 Put the heads and shells in a saucepan with the water, quartered onion and 1 bay leaf. Bring to the boil, then partly cover and simmer for 20 minutes. Strain, reserving the stock and set aside.

3 Heat the oil in a cast-iron or steel pan. (Do not use a non-stick pan.) When the oil is hot, add the flour, a little at a time, and mix to a smooth paste using a wooden spoon.

4 Cook over a medium-low heat, stirring frequently, until the Cajun roux reaches the desired colour. It will take 25–40 minutes for the roux to deepen gradually in colour from light beige to tan to a deeper, redder brown. When it reaches the colour of peanut butter, remove the pan from the heat and continue stirring until the roux has cooled and stopped cooking.

5 Melt the margarine or butter in a large heavy saucepan. Add the onions, green pepper and celery. Cook over a medium-low heat for 6–8 minutes, stirring occasionally, until the onions are softened.

6 Add the sausage and cook for 5 minutes. Stir in the okra and garlic, and cook until the okra stops producing white "threads".

7 Add the other bay leaves, thyme, salt, black and white pepper, cayenne and Tabasco sauce to taste, if desired. Mix well. Stir in 1.5 litres/2¹/₂ pints/6 cups of the prawn stock and the tomatoes. Bring to the boil, then partly cover the pan, lower the heat and simmer for about 20 minutes.

8 Whisk in the Cajun roux. Raise the heat and bring the mixture to the boil, whisking well. Lower the heat again and simmer, uncovered, for 40–50 minutes more, stirring occasionally.

9 Gently stir in the prawns and crab meat. Cook for 3–4 minutes, until the prawns turn pink. To serve, put a mound of hot rice in each serving bowl and ladle the gumbo on the top.

SOUTHERN FRIED CHICKEN

imply serve these spicy chicken pieces with fresh white bread rolls for a taste of the South.

INGREDIENTS

120ml/4fl oz/¹/₂ cup buttermilk
1.5kg/3lb chicken, cut in pieces
oil, for frying
50g/2oz/¹/₂ cup flour
15ml/1 tbsp paprika
1.5ml/¹/₄ tsp pepper
15ml/1 tbsp water

SERVES 4

1 Put the buttermilk in a bowl and add the chicken. Stir, and set aside for 5 minutes.

2 Heat a 5mm/¹/₄in layer of oil in a large frying pan over a medium-high heat. Do not let the oil overheat.

3 In a bowl or plastic bag, combine the flour, paprika and pepper. One by one, lift the chicken pieces out of the buttermilk and dip into the flour to coat all over, shaking off any excess.

4 Add the chicken pieces to the hot oil and fry for about 10 minutes until lightly browned, turning over halfway through the cooking time.

5 Reduce the heat to low and add the water to the frying pan. Cover and cook for 30 minutes, turning the pieces over at 10-minute intervals. Uncover the pan and continue cooking for about 15 minutes, until the chicken is very tender and the coating is crisp, turning every 5 minutes. Serve hot.

SAN FRANCISCO CHICKEN WINGS

C hicken wings baked in a tangy sauce create a delicious main meal. Serve with boiled potatoes and a crisp green salad.

INGREDIENTS

75ml/¹⁄₃ cup soy sauce
15ml/1 tbsp light brown sugar
15ml/1 tbsp rice vinegar
30ml/2 tbsp dry sherry
juice of 1 orange
5cm/2in strip of orange peel
1 star anise
5ml/1 tsp cornflour
50ml/2fl oz/¹⁄₄ cup water
15ml/1 tbsp chopped fresh root ginger
1.5ml/¹⁄₄ tsp Oriental chilli-garlic sauce, to taste
1.5kg/3¹⁄₂lb chicken wings (22–24), tips removed

SERVES 4

1 Preheat the oven to 200°C/400°F/Gas 6. Combine the soy sauce, brown sugar, vinegar, sherry, orange juice and peel and star anise in a saucepan. Bring to the boil over a medium heat.

2 Combine the cornflour and water in a small bowl and stir until blended. Add to the boiling soy sauce mixture, stirring well. Boil for 1 minute more, stirring constantly.

3 Remove the soy sauce mixture from the heat and stir in the chopped root ginger and chilli-garlic sauce.

4 Arrange the chicken wings, in one layer, in a large baking dish. Pour over the soy sauce mixture and stir to coat the chicken wings evenly.

5 Bake for 30–40 minutes, basting occasionally, until tender and browned. Serve the wings hot or warm.

COUNTRY MEAT LOAF

A crispy bacon shell holds this meat loaf together. Slice it thickly to serve to your guests with a fresh green vegetable and mashed potatoes.

INGREDIENTS

25g/1oz/2 tbsp butter or margarine
115g/4oz onion, finely chopped
2 garlic cloves, finely chopped
50g/2oz celery, finely chopped
450g/1lb lean minced beef
225g/8oz minced veal or lamb
225g/8oz lean minced pork
2 eggs
50g/2oz/1 cup fresh breadcrumbs
25g/1oz/¹/₂ cup chopped fresh parsley
30ml/2 tbsp chopped fresh basil
2.5ml/¹/₂ tsp fresh or dried thyme leaves
2.5ml/¹/₂ tsp salt
2.5ml/¹/₂ tsp ground black pepper
30ml/2 tbsp Worcestershire sauce
50ml/2fl oz/¹/₄ cup chilli sauce
or ketchup
6 slices streaky bacon
fresh parsley and basil leaves, to garnish

SERVES 6

1 Preheat the oven to 180°C/350°F/Gas 4. Melt the butter or margarine over a low heat. Add the onion, garlic and celery and cook for 8–10 minutes until softened. Remove from the heat and cool slightly.

2 Combine the onion, garlic and celery with all the other ingredients except the bacon. Mix together lightly, using a fork or your fingers. Do not overwork or the meat loaf will be too compact.

3 Form the meat mixture into an oval loaf. Transfer it to a shallow baking tin.

4 Lay the bacon slices across the meat loaf. Bake for 1¼ hours, basting it with the juices and bacon fat in the pan.

5 Remove the loaf from the oven and drain off the fat. Allow to stand for a few minutes before serving garnished with fresh parsley and basil leaves.

RED FLANNEL HASH

he potatoes absorb the beetroot colouring and flavour to make this a hash with a difference.

INGREDIENTS
6 slices streaky bacon
2 small onions, finely chopped
6 potatoes, boiled and diced
110g/4oz corned beef, chopped
250g/9oz cooked beetroot
(not in vinegar), diced
50ml/25fl oz/¼ cup single cream
15ml/1 tbsp chopped fresh parsley
salt and ground black pepper
fresh parsley sprigs, to garnish

SERVES 4

1 Dry fry the bacon until golden and beginning to crisp. Remove and drain on kitchen paper. Pour off all but 30ml/2 tbsp of the bacon fat in the pan, reserving the rest.

2 Cut the bacon into 1cm/½in pieces and place in a mixing bowl. Cook the onions in the bacon fat over a low heat for about 8–10 minutes until softened. Remove from the pan and add to the bacon. Mix in the potatoes, corned beef, beetroot, cream and parsley. Season with salt and pepper and mix well.

3 Heat 60ml/4 tbsp of the reserved bacon fat, or other fat, in the frying pan. Add the hash mixture, spreading it evenly over the base with a spatula. Cook over a low heat for about 15 minutes, until the base is brown. Flip the hash out on to a plate.

4 Slide the hash back into the pan and cook the other side until browned. Serve at once, garnished with fresh parsley.

PORK FAJITAS

ajitas make a wonderful meal and diners can assemble their own at the table, to ensure satisfaction.

INGREDIENTS
juice of 3 limes
90ml/6 tbsp olive oil
5ml/1 tsp dried oregano
5ml/1 tsp ground cumin
2.5ml/¹/₂ tsp red pepper flakes
675g/1¹/₂lb pork tenderloin, cut across in 7.5cm/3in pieces
2 large onions, halved and thinly sliced
1 large green pepper, seeded and thinly sliced lengthways
salt

TO SERVE
12–15 flour tortillas, warmed
tomato salsa, guacamole, soured cream, lettuce and fresh parsley

SERVES 6

1 Mix together the lime juice, 45ml/3 tbsp of the oil, oregano, cumin and red pepper flakes. Add the pork pieces and turn to coat. Cover and leave for 1 hour or chill overnight.

2 Remove the pieces of pork from the marinade. Pat them dry and season well.

3 Heat a ridged grill pan. When hot, add the pork and cook over a high heat, for 10–12 minutes, turning occasionally, until browned on all sides and cooked through.

4 Meanwhile, heat the remaining oil in a large frying pan. Add the onions and green pepper. Stir in 2.5ml/¹/₂ tsp of salt, and cook for about 15 minutes, until the vegetables are very soft, stirring occasionally. Remove and set aside.

5 Slice the pork pieces into thin strips. Add to the onion mixture and reheat briefly if necessary.

6 Spoon a little of the pork mixture on to each tortilla. Spread on some salsa, guacamole and soured cream, and roll up. Serve with extra salsa and some crisp lettuce and garnish with fresh parsley.

TURKEY BREASTS WITH TOMATO AND SWEETCORN SALSA

spicy salsa combines with grilled turkey breasts for a true taste of the Midwest.

INGREDIENTS
4 skinless, boneless turkey breast halves,
about 175g/6oz each
30ml/2 tbsp fresh lemon juice
30ml/2 tbsp olive oil
2.5ml/½ tsp ground cumin
2.5ml/½ tsp dried oregano
5ml/1 tsp coarse black pepper
salt
lettuce leaves, to serve

FOR THE SALSA
1 fresh green chilli pepper
450g/1lb tomatoes, seeded and chopped
250g/9oz/1½ cups sweetcorn kernels,
freshly cooked or thawed if frozen
3 spring onions, chopped
15ml/1 tbsp chopped fresh parsley
30ml/2 tbsp chopped fresh coriander
30ml/2 tbsp fresh lemon juice
45ml/3 tbsp olive oil
5ml/1 tsp salt

SERVES 4

1 With a meat mallet or rolling pin, pound the turkey breasts between two sheets of greaseproof paper until thin.

2 In a shallow dish, combine the lemon juice, olive oil, cumin, oregano and pepper. Add the turkey and turn to coat. Cover and leave to stand for at least 2 hours, or chill overnight.

3 For the salsa, roast the chilli over a gas flame, holding it with tongs, until charred on all sides. (Alternatively, char the skin under the grill.) Leave to cool for about 5 minutes. Wearing rubber gloves, carefully rub off the charred skin. For a milder flavour, discard the seeds. Chop the chilli finely and place in a bowl.

4 Add the remaining salsa ingredients to the chilli in the bowl and toss well to blend. Set aside.

5 Remove the turkey from the marinade. Season it lightly with salt to taste on both sides.

6 Heat a ridged grill pan. When it is hot, add the turkey breasts and cook for about 3 minutes, until browned. Turn the meat over and and grill it on the other side for 3–4 minutes more, until cooked through. Serve at once, accompanied by the salsa and crisp lettuce leaves.

CHEESEBURGERS

L oved by all kids, there is nothing to beat a homemade burger. Served with chips in a lightly toasted bun, this burger is bound together with bulgur wheat which is good for them too.

INGREDIENTS

75g/3oz/¹/₂ cup bulgur wheat
225g/8oz/2 cups minced beef
1 onion
15ml/1 tbsp chopped fresh parsley
15ml/1 tbsp tomato purée
15ml/1 tbsp grated Parmesan cheese
1 egg, lightly beaten
4 hamburger buns, lightly toasted
lettuce leaves
4 cheese slices
salt and ground black pepper
chips and ketchup, to serve
fresh parsley sprigs, to garnish

SERVES 4

1 Place the bulgur wheat in a bowl and add enough boiling water to cover. Leave to stand for 10 minutes. Drain off any excess liquid if necessary.

2 Put the minced beef into a bowl and break it up with a fork.

3 Place the onion and parsley in a food processor or blender and process for 20 seconds. Add to the beef.

4 Stir in the tomato purée and grated Parmesan cheese. Season well and add the drained bulgur wheat.

5 Stir in the beaten egg and bring the mixture together. Shape into four hamburgers with your hands. Grill for 8–10 minutes on each side under a medium heat or until cooked through.

6 Split the hamburger buns in half and place a hamburger inside each one together with some lettuce leaves. Top with a cheese slice and the hamburger bun top. Serve with chips and ketchup, garnished with fresh parsley.

BARBECUED SPARERIBS

R emember to provide finger bowls for your guests when serving spareribs – they can prove to be very messy to eat!

INGREDIENTS
1.5kg/3lb meaty pork spareribs,
in 2 pieces
120ml/4fl oz/¹/₂ cup oil
2.5ml/¹/₂ tsp paprika
crusty bread, to serve

FOR THE SAUCE
115g/4oz/¹/₂ cup light brown sugar,
firmly packed
10ml/2 tsp mustard powder
5ml/1 tsp salt
¹/₈ tsp pepper
2.5ml/¹/₂ tsp ground ginger
120ml/4fl oz/¹/₂ cup sieved
tomatoes (passata)
120ml/4fl oz/¹/₂ cup fresh orange juice
1 small onion, finely chopped
1 garlic clove, finely chopped
30ml/2 tbsp chopped fresh parsley
15ml/1 tbsp Worcestershire sauce

SERVES 4

1 Preheat the oven to 190°C/375°F/Gas 5. Arrange the ribs in one overlapping layer in a roasting tin.

2 In a small bowl, combine the oil and paprika. Brush the mixture over the spareribs. Bake for 55–60 minutes, until the ribs are slightly crisp.

3 Combine the sauce ingredients in a small pan and bring to the boil. Simmer for about 5 minutes, stirring occasionally.

4 Pour off the fat from the roasting tin. Brush the spareribs with half of the sauce and bake for 20 minutes. Turn the ribs over, brush with the remaining sauce and bake for 20 minutes longer. Cut into sections for serving with crusty bread.

CHILLI CON CARNE

A classic recipe that has become a regular feature in many homes. Simple and economical, it is one of the most popular of all minced beef recipes.

INGREDIENTS
15ml/1 tbsp oil
225g/8oz/2 cups minced beef
1 onion, quartered
5ml/1 tsp chilli powder
15g/½oz/2 tbsp flour
30ml/2 tbsp tomato purée
150ml/¼ pint/⅔ cup beef stock
200g/7oz can chopped tomatoes
200g/7oz can kidney beans, drained
1 green pepper, seeded and chopped
15ml/1 tbsp Worcestershire sauce
100g/3oz/½ cup long grain rice
salt
soured cream, to serve
chopped fresh parsley, to garnish

SERVES 4

1 Heat the oil in a large pan and fry the minced beef, onion and chilli powder for 7 minutes.

2 Add the flour and tomato purée and cook for 1 minute. Stir in the stock and tomatoes and bring to the boil.

3 Add the kidney beans, green pepper and Worcestershire sauce. Reduce the heat and simmer for 45 minutes.

4 Meanwhile, cook the rice in boiling salted water for 10–12 minutes. Drain well and spoon on to a serving plate. Spoon the chilli over the rice, add a spoonful of soured cream and garnish with parsley.

STUFFED POTATO SKINS

Customize your potato skins by adding any of your favourite herbs or spices to the potato mixture. You can just experiment to create your own variation on this dish.

INGREDIENTS

3 baking potatoes, about 375g/12oz each,
scrubbed and patted dry
15ml/1 tbsp oil
40g/1½oz/3 tbsp butter
1 onion, chopped
1 green pepper, seeded and
roughly chopped
5ml/1 tsp paprika
115g/4oz/1 cup Cheddar cheese,
roughly grated
salt and ground black pepper
crisp green salad, to serve
fresh parsley, to garnish

SERVES 6

1 Preheat the oven to 230°C/450°F/Gas 8. Brush the potatoes all over with the oil and prick them with a fork.

2 Place the potatoes in a baking dish. Bake for about 1½ hours, or until tender.

3 Meanwhile, heat the butter in a large non-stick frying pan. Add the onion and a little salt and cook over a medium heat for about 5 minutes until softened. Add the chopped green pepper and continue cooking for 2–3 minutes until it is just tender but still slightly crunchy. Stir in the paprika and set aside.

4 When the potatoes are cooked, halve them lengthways. Scoop out the flesh, keeping the pieces rough. Keep the potato skins warm.

VARIATION

For Bacon-Stuffed Potato Skins, add 25g/1oz/¼ cup chopped cooked bacon to the cooked potato flesh and vegetables. Stuff as above.

5 Preheat the grill. Add the potato flesh to the frying pan and cook over a high heat, stirring, until it is lightly browned. Season with black pepper.

6 Divide the vegetable mixture evenly among the potato skin shells.

7 Sprinkle the grated cheese over the top. Grill the potatoes for 3–5 minutes, until the cheese just melts. Serve them at once with a crisp green salad and garnish with fresh parsley.

CREAMY COLESLAW

oleslaw is a great accompaniment to any main dish. Serve this one with Southern Fried Chicken and chips for a great lunch.

INGREDIENTS
350g/12oz white cabbage, cut in wedges and cored
115g/4oz red cabbage, cored
3 spring onions, finely chopped
2 carrots, roughly grated
5ml/1 tsp sugar
30ml/2 tbsp fresh lemon juice
10ml/2 tsp white wine vinegar
120ml/4fl oz/¹⁄₂ cup soured cream
120ml/4fl oz/¹⁄₂ cup mayonnaise
4ml/³⁄₄ tsp celery seeds
salt and ground black pepper

SERVES 6

1 Slice the white and red cabbage very thinly across the leaves.

2 Place the cabbage in a mixing bowl and add the spring onions and grated carrot. Toss to combine.

3 In a small bowl, combine the sugar, lemon juice, vinegar, soured cream, mayonnaise and celery seeds.

4 Pour the mayonnaise dressing over the vegetables. Season with salt and pepper. Stir until well coated and spoon into a serving bowl.

POTATO SALAD

or a change, you could use small red potatoes to give an attractive colour to this salad.

INGREDIENTS
1.5kg/3lb small new potatoes
30ml/2 tbsp white wine vinegar
15ml/1 tbsp Dijon mustard
45ml/3 tbsp olive oil
1 red onion, finely chopped
120ml/4fl oz/¹/₂ cup mayonnaise
30ml/2 tbsp chopped fresh tarragon or
7.5ml/1¹/₂ tsp dried tarragon
¹/₂ celery stick, thinly sliced
salt and ground black pepper

SERVES 8

1 Cook the unpeeled potatoes in boiling salted water for 15–20 minutes, until just tender. Drain thoroughly.

2 In a small bowl, mix together the vinegar and mustard until the mustard dissolves. Whisk in the oil.

3 When the potatoes are cool enough to handle, use a sharp knife to slice them into a large mixing bowl.

4 Add the onion to the potatoes and pour the dressing over them. Season, then toss gently to combine. Leave to stand for at least 30 minutes.

5 Mix together the mayonnaise and tarragon. Stir into the potatoes gently along with the celery. Taste and adjust the seasoning before serving.

ASPARAGUS, SWEETCORN AND RED PEPPER QUICHE

he delicate flavours of asparagus and sweetcorn make this a heavenly quiche. Enjoy!

INGREDIENTS

185g/6¹/₂oz/1²/₃ cups flour
2.5ml/¹/₂ tsp salt
115g/4oz/³/₄ cup white vegetable fat
30–45ml/2–3 tbsp very cold water
225g/8oz fresh asparagus, woody stalks removed
25g/1oz/2 tbsp butter or margarine
1 small onion, finely chopped
1 red pepper, seeded and finely chopped
75g/3oz/¹/₂ cup drained canned sweetcorn, thawed if frozen
2 eggs
250ml/8fl oz/1 cup single cream
50g/2oz/¹/₂ cup Cheddar cheese, roughly grated
salt and ground black pepper

SERVES 6

1 Preheat the oven to 200°C/400°F/Gas 6. Sift the flour and salt into a bowl. Rub in the fat until the mixture resembles coarse breadcrumbs. Sprinkle in the cold water, 15ml/1 tbsp at a time, tossing the mixture lightly with your fingertips or a fork until the dough forms a ball when gathered together.

2 Roll out the pastry and use it to line a 25cm/10in quiche dish or loose-bottomed tart tin. Trim off excess pastry.

3 Line the pastry case with greaseproof paper and weigh it down with dry beans. Bake for 10 minutes. Remove the paper and beans and bake for about 5 minutes longer, until the pastry case is set and beige in colour. Leave to cool.

4 Trim the stem ends of eight of the asparagus spears to make them 10cm/4in long. Set aside.

5 Finely chop the asparagus trimmings and any remaining spears. Place in the bottom of the pastry case.

6 Melt the butter or margarine in a frying pan. Add the onion and red pepper and cook for about 5 minutes, until softened. Stir in the sweetcorn kernels and cook for 2 minutes longer.

7 Spoon the sweetcorn mixture over the chopped asparagus in the pastry case. In a small bowl, beat the eggs with the cream. Stir in the cheese and salt and pepper to taste. Pour into the pastry case.

8 Arrange the reserved asparagus spears like the spokes of a wheel on top of the filling. Bake for 25–30 minutes, until the filling is set.

CAESAR SALAD

 classic salad combining hard-boiled eggs with lettuce in a dressing and topped with garlic croûtons.

INGREDIENTS
2 eggs
1 garlic clove, finely chopped
2.5ml/¹/₂ tsp salt
120ml/4fl oz/¹/₂ cup olive oil
juice of 1 lemon
1.5ml/¹/₄ tsp Worcestershire sauce
1 cos lettuce, torn into bite-size pieces
40g/1¹/₂oz/¹/₂ cup grated
Parmesan cheese
ground black pepper
8 canned anchovy fillets, drained and
blotted dry on kitchen paper (optional)

FOR THE CROUTONS
1 garlic clove
1.5ml/¹/₄ tsp salt
50ml/2fl oz/¹/₄ cup olive oil
50g/2oz French bread, cubed

SERVES 4

1 Preheat the oven to 180°C/350°F/Gas 4. For the croûtons, crush the garlic with the salt in a mixing bowl and mix in the oil. Add the bread cubes to the bowl and toss to coat with the garlic oil.

2 Spread the bread cubes on a baking sheet. Bake for 20–25 minutes, until golden brown.

3 Meanwhile, put the eggs in a small pan of boiling water and simmer gently for 7 minutes. Transfer to a bowl of cold water and shell them as soon as they are cool enough to handle.

4 Mash the garlic clove with the salt in the bottom of a salad bowl. Then, very carefully whisk in the olive oil, lemon juice and Worcestershire sauce.

5 Add the lettuce to the salad bowl and toss well to coat with the dressing. Add the grated Parmesan cheese and season well with pepper. Add the croûtons and toss to combine.

6 Cut the hard-boiled eggs into quarters. Arrange on top of the salad with the anchovies, if using. Serve at once.

GUACAMOLE

T his versatile dip can be served as an accompaniment to many dishes. Try it with fajitas, tortilla chips or a selection of mixed raw vegetables.

INGREDIENTS
3 large ripe avocados
3 spring onions, finely chopped
1 garlic clove, finely chopped
15ml/1 tbsp olive oil
15ml/1 tbsp soured cream
2.5ml/¹⁄₂ tsp salt
30ml/2 tbsp fresh lemon juice
sliced mixed peppers, to serve

MAKES 475ML/16FL OZ/2 CUPS

1 Halve the avocados and remove the stones. Peel the halves. Put the avocado flesh in a large bowl.

2 Using a fork, carefully mash the avocado flesh roughly.

3 Add the spring onions, garlic, olive oil, soured cream, salt and lemon juice. Mash until well blended, but do not overwork the mixture. Small chunks of avocado should still remain. Taste the guacamole and adjust the seasoning if necessary, with more salt or lemon juice.

4 Transfer to a serving bowl. Serve at once with slices of pepper for dipping.

COOK'S TIP
Guacamole does not keep well but, if necessary, it can be stored in the fridge for a few hours. Cover the surface with clear film to prevent it from discolouring.

41

BOSTON BAKED BEANS

A bubbling casserole of haricot beans and salt pork provides a nutritious and satisfying meal for the whole family to enjoy.

INGREDIENTS
500g/1¼lb/3 cups dried haricot beans,
soaked overnight
1 bay leaf
4 cloves
2 onions
185g/6½oz/½ cup black treacle
175g/6oz/¾ cup dark brown sugar
15ml/1 tbsp Dijon mustard
5ml/1 tsp salt
5ml/1 tsp pepper
250ml/8fl oz/1 cup boiling water
225g/8oz piece salt pork

SERVES 8

1 Drain and rinse the beans. Put them in a large saucepan with the bay leaf and cover with cold water. Bring to the boil and simmer for 1½–2 hours, until tender. Drain.

2 Preheat the oven to 140°C/275°F/Gas 1. Put the beans in a large ovenproof dish. Stick two cloves into each of the onions and add them to the dish.

3 In a mixing bowl, combine the treacle, sugar, mustard, salt and pepper. Add the boiling water and stir to mix.

4 Pour this mixture over the beans. Add more water if necessary so that the beans are almost covered with liquid.

5 Blanch the piece of salt pork in boiling water for 3 minutes. Drain. Score the rind in deep cuts 1cm/½in apart. Add the salt pork to the dish and push it down just below the surface of the beans, skin-side up.

6 Cover the dish and bake in the centre of the oven for 4½–5 hours. Uncover for the last 30 minutes, so that the pork rind becomes brown and crisp. Slice or shred the pork and serve hot.

BAKED ACORN SQUASH WITH HERBS

If you can't get hold of acorn squash, make this dish with a variety available at your local greengrocer – the result will be just as good.

INGREDIENTS

2 acorn squash
90ml/6 tbsp chopped fresh chives, thyme,
basil and parsley
50g/2oz/4 tbsp butter or margarine
salt and ground black pepper
mixed fresh herbs, to garnish

SERVES 4

1 Cut each squash in half crossways and scoop out the seeds and stringy fibres. If necessary, cut a small slice off the base of each squash half so it sits level.

2 Preheat the oven to 190°C/375°F/Gas 5. Divide the chopped herbs into four and spoon into the hollows in the squash halves.

3 Top each half with butter or margarine and season with salt and pepper.

4 Arrange the squash halves in a shallow baking dish large enough to hold them in one layer. Pour boiling water into the bottom of the dish to a depth of about 2.5cm/1in. Cover the squash loosely with a piece of foil.

5 Bake for ¾–1 hour, until the squash is tender when tested with a fork. Serve hot, keeping the halves upright, garnished with fresh herbs.

MACARONI CHEESE

T he crusty cheesy topping makes this Macaroni Cheese just that bit more special.

INGREDIENTS

115g/4oz/1 cup elbow macaroni
50g/2oz/4 tbsp butter or margarine
25g/1oz/¼ cup flour
600ml/1 pint/2½ cups milk
175g/6oz/1½ cups Cheddar
cheese, grated
30ml/2 tbsp finely chopped fresh parsley
65g/2½oz/1 cup dry breadcrumbs
40g/1½oz/½cup grated
Parmesan cheese
salt and ground black pepper

SERVES 4

1 Preheat the oven to 180°C/350°F/Gas 4. Grease a 25cm/10in gratin dish, then cook the macaroni in a large pan of boiling salted water until just tender to the bite (check the directions on the packet for timing). Drain the pasta well.

2 Melt the butter or margarine in a pan. Add the flour and cook for 2 minutes, stirring, then stir in the milk. Bring to the boil, stirring constantly, and simmer for about 5 minutes, until thickened.

3 Remove the pan from the heat. Add the cooked macaroni, Cheddar cheese and parsley to the sauce and mix well. Season with salt and pepper.

4 Transfer the mixture to the prepared gratin dish, spreading it out evenly with a spoon.

5 Mix the breadcrumbs and Parmesan cheese together with a fork and sprinkle over the macaroni.

6 Bake for 30–35 minutes, until the top is golden brown and the macaroni mixture is bubbling.

EGGS BENEDICT

f possible, use free-range eggs for this dish as they have a vibrant yellow colour.

INGREDIENTS
3 egg yolks
30ml/2 tbsp fresh lemon juice
1.5ml/¹/₄ tsp salt
115g/4oz/8 tbsp butter
30ml/2 tbsp single cream
5ml/1 tsp vinegar
4 fresh eggs
2 muffins or 4 rounds of bread
butter, for spreading
2 thick slices of cooked ham
white pepper
fresh chives, to garnish
lettuce and tomato salad, to serve

SERVES 4

1 Blend the yolks, lemon juice and salt in a food processor or blender for 15 seconds.

2 Melt the butter until it bubbles (do not let it brown). With the motor running, pour the hot butter into the food processor or blender through the feed tube in a slow, steady stream. Turn off the machine as soon as all the butter has been added.

3 Scrape the sauce into the top of a double boiler or into a bowl set over a pan of just-simmering water. Stir for 2–3 minutes, until thickened. (If the sauce curdles, whisk in 15ml/1 tbsp of boiling water.) Stir in the cream and season with white pepper. Keep warm over the hot water.

4 Bring a shallow saucepan of water to the boil. Stir in the vinegar. Break two of the eggs into separate cups, then slide them carefully into the gently simmering water. Delicately turn the white around the yolk with a slotted spoon. Cook until the eggs are set to your taste, for about 3–4 minutes. Remove to kitchen paper to drain. Repeat with the remaining eggs. Very gently cut any ragged edges off the eggs with a small knife or scissors.

5 While the eggs are poaching, split and toast the muffins or toast the bread slices. Butter while still warm.

6 Cut the ham slices in half crossways and brown them in butter if you wish. Place them on each muffin half or slice of toast. Trim the ham to fit neatly. Place an egg on each ham-topped muffin. Spoon the warm sauce over the eggs, garnish with chives and serve with a lettuce and tomato salad.

CORNBREAD

S quares of golden bread served with butter, or just on their own, are bound to be a hit with anyone feeling peckish around the home.

INGREDIENTS
2 eggs, lightly beaten
250ml/8fl oz/1 cup buttermilk
115g/4oz/1 cup plain flour
115g/4oz/1 cup cornmeal
10ml/2 tsp baking powder
2.5ml/¹/₂ tsp salt
15ml/1 tbsp sugar
115g/4oz/1 cup mature Cheddar cheese, grated
175g/6oz/1 cup sweetcorn kernels, cut from 2 ears of fresh corn or thawed if frozen

MAKES 9

1 Preheat the oven to 200°C/400°F/Gas 6. Grease a 23cm/9in square baking tin.

2 Put the eggs and buttermilk in a small mixing bowl and whisk until well combined. Set aside.

3 In another bowl, stir together the flour, cornmeal, baking powder, salt and sugar. Pour in the egg mixture and stir with a wooden spoon until just combined. Mix in the cheese and sweetcorn.

4 Pour the batter into the prepared pan. Bake for about 25 minutes, until a skewer inserted in the centre comes out clean.

5 Unmould the cornbread on to a wire rack and leave to cool completely. Cut into 7.5cm/3in squares for serving.

PIZZA

dapt this recipe to suit your tastes: let your imagination run wild with a topping of your choice!

INGREDIENTS
500g/1¹/₄lb/5 cups plain flour
5ml/1 tsp salt
10ml/2 tsp dried yeast
300ml/10fl oz/1¹/₄ cups lukewarm water
about 50ml/2fl oz/¹/₄ cup olive oil

FOR THE TOPPING
tomato sauce
grated Cheddar cheese
olives and herbs

MAKES 2

1 Mix the flour and salt and make a well in the centre. Add the yeast, water and 30ml/2 tbsp of olive oil. Leave for 15 minutes.

2 Stir the dough until it just holds together. Knead until smooth and elastic. Avoid adding too much flour while kneading.

3 Brush the inside of a bowl with oil. Place the dough in the bowl and roll around to coat with the oil. Cover with a plastic bag and leave to rise in a warm place for about 45 minutes, until doubled in volume.

4 Divide the dough into two balls. Preheat the oven to 200°C/400°F/Gas 6.

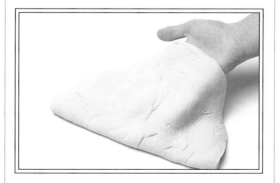

5 Roll each ball into a 25cm/10in circle. Flip the circles over and on to your palm. Set each circle on the work surface and rotate, stretching the dough as you turn, until it is about 30cm/12in across.

6 Brush two pizza tins or baking sheets with oil. Place the dough circles in the tins and push the edges up slightly to form a rim. Brush with oil.

7 Cover with the topping and bake for 10–12 minutes until golden.

WHOLEMEAL BANANA NUT LOAF

Serve thick slices of this deliciously moist loaf with mugs of steaming hot coffee for the perfect mid-morning snack.

INGREDIENTS

115g/4oz/¹/₂ cup butter, at room temperature
115g/4oz/¹/₂ cup caster sugar
2 eggs, at room temperature
115g/4oz/1 cup plain flour
5ml/1 tsp bicarbonate of soda
1.5ml/¹/₄ tsp salt
5ml/1 tsp ground cinnamon
50g/2oz/¹/₂ cup wholemeal flour
3 large ripe bananas
5ml/1 tsp vanilla essence
50g/2oz/¹/₂ cup chopped walnuts

MAKES 1 LOAF

1 Preheat the oven to 180°C/350°F/Gas 4. Carefully line the bottom and sides of a 23 x 13cm/9 x 5in loaf tin with greaseproof paper and grease the paper.

2 With an electric mixer, cream the butter and sugar together until light and fluffy.

3 Add the eggs, one at a time, beating well after each addition.

4 Sift the plain flour, bicarbonate of soda, salt and cinnamon over the butter mixture and stir to blend. Stir in the wholemeal flour.

5 With a fork, mash the bananas to a purée, then stir it into the mixture. Stir in the vanilla essence and walnuts.

6 Pour the mixture into the prepared tin and spread it level.

7 Bake for 50–60 minutes, until a skewer inserted in the centre comes out clean. Leave to stand for 10 minutes before transferring to a wire rack to cool.

BLUEBERRY MUFFINS

T hese muffins are so delicious that they certainly won't be allowed to hang around on the serving plate for very long.

INGREDIENTS
115g/4oz/1 cup plain flour
15ml/1 tbsp baking powder
1/8 tsp salt
175g/6oz/1/3 cup light brown sugar
1 egg
175ml/6fl oz/3/4 cup milk
45ml/3 tbsp oil
10ml/2 tsp ground cinnamon
115g/4oz/1 cup fresh blueberries,
or thawed

MAKES 8

VARIATION
Use other fruit instead of blueberries: blackcurrants, blackberries, cherries and raspberries all work just as well.

1 Preheat the oven to 190°C/375°F/Gas 5. Grease a muffin tin.

2 With an electric mixer, beat all the ingredients except the blueberries together until smooth.

3 Using a wooden spoon, gently fold in the blueberries to the creamed mixture.

4 Spoon the batter into the muffin tin, filling eight cups two-thirds full. Bake for about 25 minutes or until a skewer inserted in the centre of a muffin comes out clean.

5 Leave to cool in the tin on a wire rack for 10 minutes, then unmould the muffins on to a wire rack and allow to cool.

HAZELNUT BROWNIES

very chocoholic loves a brownie, and this recipe will prove no exception for them.

INGREDIENTS

50g/2oz plain dark chocolate
65g/2¹/₂oz/5 tbsp butter or margarine
225g/8oz/1 cup sugar
50g/2oz/7 tbsp plain flour
2.5ml/¹/₂ tsp baking powder
2 eggs, beaten
2.5ml/¹/₂ tsp vanilla essence
115g/4oz/1 cup skinned hazelnuts,
roughly chopped

MAKES 9

1 Preheat the oven to 180°C/350°F/Gas 4. Grease a 20cm/8in square baking tin. In a bowl set over a pan of simmering water, or in a double boiler, melt the chocolate and butter or margarine. Remove from the heat.

2 Add the sugar, flour, baking powder, eggs, vanilla essence and half the hazelnuts to the melted mixture. Stir well with a wooden spoon.

3 Pour the batter into the prepared tin. Bake for 10 minutes, then sprinkle the reserved hazelnuts over the top. Return to the oven and continue baking for about 25 minutes, until firm to the touch.

4 Set the tin on a wire rack and leave to cool for 10 minutes, then unmould it on to the rack and leave to cool completely. Cut the brownies into squares for serving.

CHOCOLATE CHIP AND MACADAMIA NUT BISCUITS

plate of freshly baked biscuits makes a welcome afternoon snack for everybody.

INGREDIENTS

115g/4oz/1 cup flour

5ml/1 tsp baking powder

1.5ml/¼ tsp salt

75g/3oz/6 tbsp butter or margarine

115g/4oz/½ cup granulated sugar

50g/2oz/¼ cup light brown sugar

1 egg

5ml/1 tsp vanilla essence

130g/4½oz/¾ cup chocolate chips

175g/6oz/½ cup macadamia
nuts, chopped

MAKES 36

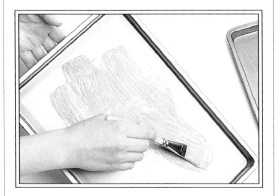

1 Preheat the oven to 180°C/350°F/Gas 4. Grease two or three baking sheets.

2 Sift the flour, baking powder and salt in a small bowl. Set aside.

3 With an electric mixer, cream the butter or margarine and sugars together. Beat in the egg and vanilla essence. Add the flour mixture and beat well with the mixer set on low speed.

4 Stir in the chocolate chips and half the macadamia nuts using a wooden spoon.

5 Drop the mixture by teaspoons on to the prepared baking sheets, to form 2cm/¾in mounds. Space the biscuits well apart as they will spread.

6 Flatten each biscuit lightly with a wet fork. Sprinkle the remaining macadamia nuts on the top and press them lightly into the surface.

7 Bake for 10–12 minutes, until golden brown. With a fish slice, transfer the biscuits to a wire rack to cool.

COOK'S TIP
Use any kind of chocolate chips you like for these biscuits: white, milk, plain or a mixture.

PUMPKIN PIE

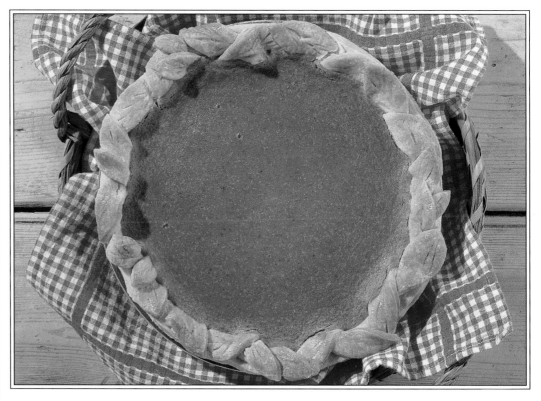

raditionally served at Thanksgiving, this pie is worth making at any time – whatever the celebration.

INGREDIENTS
450g/1lb/2 cups cooked or
canned pumpkin
250ml/8fl oz/1 cup whipping cream
2 eggs
115g/4oz/¹/₂ cup dark brown sugar
60ml/4 tbsp light corn syrup
7.5ml/1¹/₂ tsp ground cinnamon
5ml/1 tsp ground ginger
1.5ml/¹/₄ tsp ground cloves
2.5ml/¹/₂ tsp salt

FOR THE PASTRY
375g/12oz/3 cups flour
2.5ml/¹/₂ tsp salt
75g/3oz/6 tbsp cold butter, diced
75g/3oz/6 tbsp cold white vegetable
fat, diced
45–60ml/3–4 tbsp very cold water

SERVES 8

1 For the pastry, sift the flour and salt and rub in the fats until it resembles coarse breadcrumbs. Stir in enough water to bind. Gather into a ball, wrap in greaseproof paper and chill for 20 minutes.

2 Roll out the dough to 3mm/⅛in thick. Transfer to a 23cm/9in pie dish. Trim off the overhang. Roll out the trimmings and cut into leaf shapes. Moisten the edge of the pastry with a brush dipped in water.

3 Arrange the pastry leaves around the edge. Chill for 20 minutes. Meanwhile, preheat the oven to 200°C/400°F/Gas 6.

4 Prick the bottom of the pastry with a fork and line with crumpled greaseproof paper. Fill with dry beans and bake for 12 minutes. Remove the paper and beans and bake for 6–8 minutes more, until golden. Reduce the heat to 190°C/375°F/Gas 5.

5 Beat together the pumpkin, cream, eggs, sugar, corn syrup, spices and salt. Pour into the pastry shell and bake the pie for about 40 minutes, until set.

PECAN TART

erve this scrumptious tart warm, accompanied by ice cream or whipped cream, if wished.

INGREDIENTS
3 eggs
⅛ tsp salt
200g/7oz/scant 1 cup dark brown sugar
120ml/4fl oz/8 tbsp golden syrup
30ml/2 tbsp fresh lemon juice
75g/3oz/6 tbsp butter, melted
150g/5oz/1¼ cups chopped pecan nuts
50g/2oz/½ cup pecan nut halves

FOR THE PASTRY
175g/6oz/1½ cups plain flour
15ml/1 tbsp caster sugar
5ml/1 tsp baking powder
2.5ml/½ tsp salt
75g/3oz/6 tbsp cold unsalted butter, diced
1 egg yolk
45–60ml/3–4 tbsp whipping cream

SERVES 8

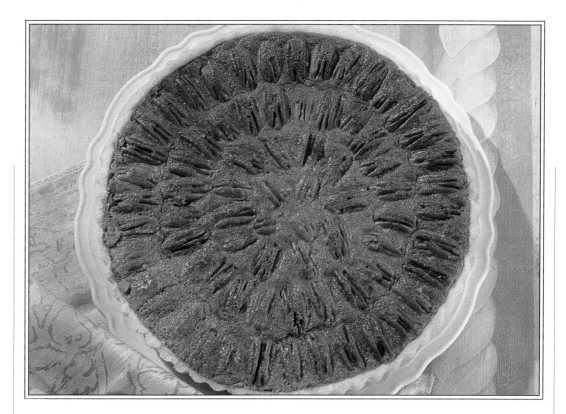

1 For the pastry, sift the flour, caster sugar, baking powder and salt into a mixing bowl. Add the butter and cut it in with a pastry blender until the mixture resembles coarse breadcrumbs.

2 In another bowl, beat together the egg yolk and cream until blended.

3 Pour the cream mixture into the flour mixture and stir in with a fork.

4 Gently gather the pastry into a ball. On a lightly floured surface, roll out to 3mm/⅛in thick and transfer to a 23cm/9in pie dish. Trim off the overhang and flute the edge with your fingers. Chill for at least 30 minutes.

5 Preheat the oven to 200°C/400°F/Gas 6, with a baking sheet on the centre shelf.

6 In a bowl, lightly whisk the eggs and salt. Add the sugar, golden syrup, lemon juice and butter. Mix well and stir in the chopped pecan nuts.

7 Pour the mixture into the pastry case and arrange the pecan halves in concentric circles on top.

8 Bake for 10 minutes. Reduce the heat to 160°C/325°F/Gas 3 and continue baking for 25 minutes more. Allow to cool in the dish on a wire rack, and serve.

APPLE PIE

ou just can't beat a homemade apple pie, and this one is sure to be a regular feature on your table.

INGREDIENTS
900g/2lb tart apples
15ml/1 tbsp fresh lemon juice
5ml/1 tsp vanilla essence
115g/4oz/¹⁄₂ cup granulated sugar
2.5ml/¹⁄₂ tsp ground cinnamon
20g/³⁄₄oz/1¹⁄₂ tbsp butter or margarine
1 egg yolk
10ml/2 tsp single cream

FOR THE PASTRY
225g/8oz/2 cups plain flour
5ml/1 tsp salt
115g/4oz/¹⁄₂ cup white vegetable fat
60–75ml/4–5 tbsp very cold water
5ml/1 tsp quick-cooking tapioca

SERVES 8

1 Preheat the oven to 230°C/450°F/Gas 8. For the pastry, sift the flour and salt into a bowl and rub in the fat until the mixture resembles coarse breadcrumbs.

2 Sprinkle in the water, 15ml/1 tbsp at a time, tossing lightly with your fingertips or a fork until the dough forms a ball.

3 Divide the dough in half and shape each half into a ball. On a lightly floured surface, roll out one of the balls to a circle about 30cm/12in across.

4 Use the pastry to line a 23cm/9in pie dish, easing it in and being careful not to stretch it. Trim off the excess pastry and use the trimmings for decorating. Sprinkle the tapioca over the bottom of the pastry case.

5 Roll out the remaining dough to a 3mm/¹⁄₈in thickness. Using a sharp knife, cut out eight large leaf shapes. Cut the trimmings into smaller leaf shapes. Score the leaves with the back of the knife to mark veins.

6 Peel, core and slice the apples into a bowl and toss with the lemon juice, vanilla essence, sugar and cinnamon. Fill the pastry case with the apple mixture and dot with the butter or margarine.

7 Arrange the large pastry leaves in a decorative pattern on top of the apples. Decorate the edges with the smaller leaves.

8 Mix together the egg yolk and cream and brush over the leaves to glaze them.

9 Bake the pie for 10 minutes, then reduce the heat to 180°C/350°F/Gas 4 and continue baking for 35–45 minutes, until the pastry is golden brown. Serve hot or, if you prefer, leave the pie to cool in the dish, set on a wire rack.

CHOCOLATE ICE CREAM

An easy-to-make dessert, this ice cream can be prepared a few days in advance and then brought out of the freezer when needed.

INGREDIENTS

475ml/16fl oz/2 cups whipping cream
3 egg yolks
350ml/12fl oz/1½ cups sweetened
condensed milk
20ml/4 tsp vanilla essence
12 bourbon biscuits, roughly crushed

MAKES 1·7 LITRES/ 3 PINTS

1 Line a 900g/2lb loaf tin with foil, leaving enough overhang to cover the top.

2 In a mixing bowl, whip the cream until soft peaks form. Set aside.

3 In another mixing bowl, beat the egg yolks until thick and pale. Stir in the sweetened condensed milk and vanilla essence. Fold in the crushed biscuits and whipped cream.

4 Pour the ice cream mixture into the prepared loaf tin. Cover it well with the foil overhang and freeze for about 6 hours, until it is firm.

5 To serve, remove the ice cream from the tin and peel off the foil. Cut into thin slices with a sharp knife.

CLASSIC CHEESECAKE

his baked cheesecake has a tangy lemon taste. Serve it with whipped cream for a divine dessert.

INGREDIENTS
50g/2oz/³/₄ cup digestive
biscuits, crushed
900g/2lb/4 cups full-fat soft cheese, at
room temperature
275g/10oz/1¹/₄ cups caster sugar
grated rind of 1 lemon
45ml/3 tbsp fresh lemon juice
5ml/1 tsp vanilla essence
4 eggs, at room temperature

SERVES 8

1 Preheat the oven to 160°C/325°F/Gas 3. Grease a 20cm/8in springform tin. Line it with a round of foil about 10cm/4in larger than the diameter of the tin. Press it up the sides to seal tightly.

2 Sprinkle the biscuit crumbs in the base of the tin. Press to form an even layer.

3 Beat the cream cheese until smooth. Add the sugar, lemon rind and juice and the vanilla essence, and beat until blended. Add the eggs, one at a time, and beat just enough to blend thoroughly.

4 Pour the cheesecake mixture into the prepared tin. Set the tin in a larger baking tin and pour enough hot water into the outer tin to come 2.5cm/1in up the sides of the cheesecake tin.

5 Bake for about 1½ hours, until the top of the cheesecake is golden brown. Leave to cool in the tin.

6 Run a knife around the edge to loosen, then remove the springform tin. Leave the cheesecake on the base and chill for at least 4 hours before serving.

DEVIL'S FOOD CAKE

ot a cake for anyone counting calories, this chocolate delight is a real tea-time treat.

INGREDIENTS
115g/4oz plain dark chocolate
300ml/¹/₂ pint/1¹/₄ cups milk
225g/8oz/1 cup light brown sugar
1 egg yolk
250g/9oz/2¹/₄ cups self-raising flour
5ml/1 tsp baking soda
2.5ml/¹/₂ tsp salt
150g/5oz/³/₄ cup butter or margarine,
at room temperature
225g/8oz/1¹/₃ cups granulated sugar
3 eggs
5ml/1 tsp vanilla essence

FOR THE ICING
225g/8oz plain dark chocolate
175ml/6fl oz/³/₄ cup soured cream
1.5ml/¹/₄ tsp salt

SERVES 10

1 Preheat the oven to 180°C/350°F/Gas 4. Line two 20–23cm/8–9in round cake tins with greaseproof paper.

2 In a heatproof bowl set over a pan of barely simmering water, or in a double boiler, combine the chocolate and all but 60ml/4 tbsp of the milk with the brown sugar and egg yolk. Cook, stirring, until smooth and thickened. Set aside to cool.

3 Meanwhile, sift the flour, baking soda, and salt into a small bowl and set aside.

4 With an electric mixer, cream the butter or margarine with the granulated sugar until light and fluffy. Beat in the whole eggs, one at a time. Mix in the vanilla essence.

5 On a low speed, beat the flour mixture into the butter mixture alternately with the remaining milk, beginning and ending with flour.

6 Pour in the cooled chocolate mixture and mix until just combined.

7 Divide the cake batter evenly between the two tins. Bake for 30–40 minutes, until a skewer inserted in the centre comes out clean.

8 Allow to cool in the tins on wire racks for 10 minutes, then unmould the cakes on to the wire racks and cool completely.

9 For the icing, melt the chocolate in a heatproof bowl set over a pan of barely simmering water, or in the top of a double boiler. Remove the bowl from the heat and stir in the soured cream and salt. Leave to cool slightly.

10 Set one cake on a serving plate and spread it with a third of the chocolate icing. Place the second cake on top. Spread the remaining icing all over the top and sides of the cake, swirling it to make a decorative finish.

INDEX